Gratefully presented to

Jan Butcheri
with Love & admiration

by

Krissy DeMart

on

March 17, 1999

Happy Birthday — to one of the best of Teachers I've ever known!

THE
TEACHER'S
APPRECIATION
BOOK
OF WIT & WISDOM

Compiled by Anna Trimiew

Harold Shaw Publishers
Wheaton, Illinois

CONTENTS

Teachers at Work

The Art of Teaching. 8

A+ Advice 13

Excellence Behind the Desk 18

Friendship 24

Voices from the Classroom

Among the Children 29

Bringing Out the Best 35

Let the Teacher Teach 41

Beginnings and Endings. 47

School Life

From Reading to Recess.............................. 54

Principals, Parents, and PTA....................... 60

Tales Out of School 65

Celebrations...................................... 70

Potpourri

Wise and Witty Sayings 76

Stickers and Other Rewards 81

Helpful Hints 87

Faith, Hope, and a Sense of Humor 91

TEACHERS
AT
WORK

The Art of Teaching

Begin school as if you had just heard good news and took pleasure in imparting [it], and keep this up all day.

Abbie G. Hall, Points Picked Up: One Hundred Hints in How to Manage a School

Train up a child in the way he should go [and in keeping with his individual gift or bent], and when he is old he will not depart from it.

Proverbs 22:6, AMP

All children—whatever their personality type or temperament—need to feel that they are experts in some area. Lucky the children whose parents [and teachers] perceive their interests, their strengths, and their learning styles and then make it possible for the children to develop their own gifts in their own ways!

The word *education* means "to draw out; to lead." It does not imply changing children into something they are not. Instead it means taking children as they are and using their inclinations, strengths, and preferences in order to draw out from them the very best that they can give.

LaVonne Neff, One of a Kind

Certainly, the main elements of teaching—order, interest, spirit, and, we must add a fourth, discipline—are as inseparable from and dependent on one another as fire, water, air, and earth were to the ancients as the building materials of the universe.

Eric W. Johnson, Teaching School

As a general rule, teachers teach more by what they are than by what they say.

Anonymous

Be convinced that the subjects and skills you teach are important to the lives, needs, and interests of your students. If you aren't, change what you are teaching or change jobs. Your own interest and conviction are contagious; so are your boredom and indecision.

Johnson, Teaching School

The mediocre teacher tells. The good teacher explains. The superior teacher demonstrates. The great teacher inspires.

Anonymous

"I am a teacher," she said to the class on this first day. "A teacher is someone who leads. There is no magic here. Mrs. Collins is no miracle worker. I do not walk on water, I do not part the sea. I just love children and work harder than a lot of people, and so will you."

Marva Collins and Civia Tamarkin, Marva Collins' Way

Only be careful, and watch yourselves closely so that you do not forget the things your eyes have seen or let them slip from your heart as long as you live. Teach them to your children and to their children after them.

Deuteronomy 4:9

"That teacher in the movies really cared. Because he gave up a good Job Just teach kids that was given him a hard time at frist. But, they come through. He gave up his spare time Just to help them, he gave up his summer without getting payed Just to help them. I can't believe any one or any teacher will ever do that. But he did. I wist I had a teacher like that."

Student's comments on the movie Stand and Deliver,
quoted by Emily Sachar in Shut Up and Let the Lady Teach

Happy and blessed is that person whom truth teacheth and informeth.

Thomas à Kempis

To teach is not to simplify every step until there is no real work for the child to do.

Hall, Points Picked Up

I talked. I talked and talked—as if I had never spoken before in all the years of my life; as if I had never uttered words before in all the classrooms I had attended. Faces turned to me. The teacher stood behind his desk, listening.

Chaim Potok, Davita's Harp

To identify teaching as an art should not lead one to conclude that formal preparation is not required. The aptitudes that lead to success in the classroom will not spring to full fruition of their own accord. Neither will the talents of painter or poet. Only after repeated exposure to the demands of the art and systematic development of the latent but recognizable qualifying abilities will that person be ready to engage in the art to which he has been called. Jesus Himself, called Teacher by His disciples, spent thirty years in preparation for His brief earthly ministry.

Norman de Jong, Education in the Truth

The essence of teaching is to make learning contagious, to have one idea spark another.

Collins and Tamarkin, Marva Collins' Way

My God, you are always close to me. In obedience to you, I must now apply myself to outward things. Yet, as I do so, I pray that you will give me the grace of your presence. And to this end I ask that you will assist my work, receive its fruits as an offering to you, and all the while direct all my affections to you.

Brother Lawrence

A+ Advice

"Mrs. Sachar, if you's gonna teach 8-1, you's gotta know how to do it.
You don't let the girls sit by the boys. You don't call on kids whose
hands ain't raised. You don't let kids be turning in work late. And you
teach us stuff for the citywide."

Student quoted in Sachar, Shut Up and Let the Lady Teach

Now, a teacher can be Mary Martin, Meryl Streep, and Charlie Chaplin
all rolled into one, but no child will learn in a threatening or hostile at-
mosphere. Children must feel safe in a classroom. So, while using his or
her acting skills, a teacher must also engage in policework. Teachers discipline, negotiate, restrain, get tough with, ease up on and generally pro-
vide their own thin blue line between civilization and chaos.

Patti Greenberg Wollman, Behind the Playdough Curtain

Never confront a student in front of his classmates. You will always lose.
He will always win.

Seventh-grade dean quoted in Sachar, Shut Up and Let the Lady Teach

Mrs. Brown went crazy when she saw my babies swarming over the playground before the time designated in the sacred rule book. I convinced her that Peter was a scholar of some renown, a gifted wanderer who traveled the country demonstrating the joys of soccer to rural children. He would even teach her class if she so desired—but she insisted indignantly that her class studied more important things than games. "You don't learn a thing by having fun. You gotta work. You gotta work."

Pat Conroy, The Water Is Wide

Teach me to do your will, for you are my God. Let your good spirit lead me on a level path.

Psalm 143:10, NRSV

She will try to be patient this year: give the class a little more time to settle down when they come in from recess, go a bit slower teaching long division and percentages, and not be so quick to jump to conclusions whenever trouble arises.

Phyllis Reynolds Naylor, Getting Along with Your Teachers

When offering helpful advice, make it a small helping.

Anonymous

The first Christians were taught by Jesus, who educated them in the true sense of the word *educare,* "to lead out." The main method of learning was for the community of disciples to follow their mentor or rabbi.

Dieter T. Hessel, Social Ministry

Religious education, both in the Hebrew and Christian past, had to do with life and living; its motivating force then as now is love . . . both the holiness code and the early catechetical teaching of the church was modeled on love toward God and love toward fellow persons. This brings together both content and action.

Robert E. Webber, Common Roots

Mr. Jenkins walked inside the giant U pattern of their desks, placing a little bag of M&M's on each desk. He caught David's wrist as a piece of candy headed for his mouth. "Remember what we discussed before recess, children. I don't want you to eat your M&M's. I want you to count them by color and make your graph. Next, we'll make a class M&M's graph. After that, we get to eat our Halloween treats."

Susan Clymer, There's a Hamster in My Lunchbox

How good is a timely word!

Proverbs 15:23, NIV

Those who can, teach. Those who can't, go into some less significant line of work.

Unknown

Allow yourself to fail, to forgive failure, and to learn from failures. You won't be right all of the time, you know, but God can use you, even in your weakness to serve his purposes. Whether you are new . . . or not, your starting point must be the realization that you are the instrument and God is the strength of your teaching. Ask him, therefore, to renew you daily—even hourly—that you may serve him well. Your commitment to be God's tool will change your focus from performance to praise.

Lorna Van Gilst, Christian Educators Journal (Oct/Nov 1989)

Our vision for education has always been to actively engage students in content, application, and calling. . . . We expect our students to use their knowledge to serve God and their neighbor.

Robert Thayer, school administrator, quoted in Christian Home & School (Jan/Feb 1995)

Both students and teachers need to treat each other with the same consideration and respect that they expect for themselves.

Naylor, Getting Along with Your Teachers

Character grows in the soil of experience, with the fertilization of example, the moisture of desire, and the sunshine of satisfaction.

Anonymous

Just as a teacher knows his or her own family members, he or she must know the students, their needs and their interests. Each child is unique.

Collins and Tamarkin, Marva Collins' Way

O God . . . Save us from slipshod or dishonest thinking. Forbid that we should turn away from any question, either because we do not know, or because we fear to give, the answer. . . . Strengthen us to read and think and work with courage and humility, confident that if we seek the truth we shall not lack the guidance of thy Spirit; through Jesus Christ our Lord.

A New Prayer Book

Excellence Behind the Desk

Father, today I felt your presence in the classroom. By faith I know that you are always there, But thank you for those times which *confirm* that in you we live and move and have our being.

Elspeth Campbell Murphy, Chalkdust: Prayer Meditations for Teachers

The world seldom notices who the teachers are; but civilization depends on what they do and what they say.

Anonymous

I tried to make my classes a stimulating experience for my students . . . life experiences, creative experiences. I tried to get them to drop prejudices and conditioned responses from their thinking. In essence, I tried to teach them to embrace life openly, to reflect upon its mysteries, rejoice in its surprises, and to reject its cruelties.

Pat Conroy, The Water Is Wide

Chris had a recurrent fantasy about waking up one day to find that a former student had become an admirable and famous personage. She felt ready to settle for something less grandiose. She hoped for confident, "well-adjusted" children. But Judith gave her one of the best feelings she had experienced in her fourteen years of teaching, the sensation that came from knowing that she had a child in the room who, with a little luck and guidance, would certainly surpass her.

Kidder, Among Schoolchildren

Good teachers care whether students learn. They challenge all students, even those who are less capable, and then help them to meet the challenge.

Teacher quoted in Lisa Delpit, Other People's Children

Light another person's candle by your own and you will not lose any of the brilliancy by what the other gains.

Jo Petty, Words of Silver and Gold

Still others have a gift for caring for God's people as a shepherd does his sheep, leading and teaching them in the ways of God.

Ephesians 4:11, TLB

Good teachers push students to think, to make their own decisions.

Quoted by Lisa Delpit in Other People's Children

If you have an idea that you really believe in, don't let anything stop you from implementing it. Just create a concrete plan and stay true to your vision and move forward.

Wendy Kopp

At the end of the semester, we gave "Academy awards" for academic performance, good behavior, perfect attendance, and overall improvement. The awards were simple paper certificates created on one of the computers in our school lab, but the kids accepted them as though they had been sent directly from the White House. For many of them, it was the first time in their lives that they had ever received positive recognition from school.

LouAnne Johnson, My Posse Don't Do Homework

It's not so much what is poured into the student, but what is planted, that really counts.

Anonymous

Good teachers are not bound to books and instructional materials, but connect all learning to real life.

Teacher quoted in Lisa Delpit, Other People's Children

Success is due less to ability than to zeal.

Petty, Words of Silver and Gold

Smart classrooms shift the emphasis from teaching to learning. Education is what takes place in the mind of the students. In smart schools the teacher does not do the learning any more than a coach scores goals or shoots baskets. He or she is the facilitator, the manager of instruction, who creates the proper learning context and helps the student to take responsibility for his or her own learning. It is the student who does the real "work" of the classroom.

Edward B. Fiske, Smart Schools, Smart Kids

Besides being wise, the Teacher also taught the people knowledge, weighing and studying and arranging many proverbs. The Teacher sought to find pleasing words, and he wrote words of truth plainly.

Ecclesiastes 12:9-10, NRSV

Father, today it all felt so *right.* The children were joyously absorbed in what they were learning, and I moved among them full of the satisfaction of a job well done.

Murphy, Chalkdust

Children need to know how to work and how to act as a learner and as a student in school. Basically, this means they need to know how to get a job done. . . . Knowing how to work results from . . . being shown patiently how to tackle the job.

Marjorie R. Simic et al., The Confident Learner

Teach with a servant attitude rather than an authoritarian one.

Joan M. Dungey

Education is about habits of the mind.

Theodore R. Sizer

God give us grace to realize that education is not simply *doing* the things we like, *studying* the tasks that appeal to us, or wandering in the world of thought *whither* and *where* we will. . . . It is the *unpleasant* task, the *hard* lesson . . . that often leads to knowledge and power and good.

W. E. B. Du Bois, Prayers for Dark People

Unable to think of an inspirational topic for journal writing, I told the kids to make the final essay a free write—they could write whatever was one their minds. One of the Spanish boys, Bryant Majernik from Argentina, wrote:

"I don't know what is in my brain. I can't see anything, is like a white wall. But I feel something, is something strong and deep. That is that I want to tell you, and thank you for all. For gave me your time and taught me all that I know in English. Thank you."

I taped Bryant's note up over my desk and once again shoved my résumé back into the drawer.

Johnson, My Posse Don't Do Homework

Give me the ability to see good things in unexpected places and talents in unexpected people. Give me the grace to tell them so.

Author unknown

I love children and I love to teach. And when I see them learning, when I see them getting it—it keeps me going year after year.

Emily Cox, teacher

Friendship

Life is made up, not of great sacrifices or duties, but of little things, in which smiles and kindness and small obligations, given habitually, are what win and preserve the heart and secure comfort.

Sir H. Davy

One of my pleasures, and the source of much of my early knowledge, was the lunch period I shared with my colleagues. . . . That hour and fifteen minutes was an invigorating and extremely fruitful break in the middle of the day . . . it took most of us perhaps fifteen minutes, at most a half hour, to eat our lunch. That left an hour to simply sit and talk with one another—to talk about the children, about our classes, about *teaching*.

Madeline Cartwright and Michael D'Orso, For the Children

Without sincerity, there is neither love, friendship, nor virtue in the world.

Joseph Addison

Friendship is the melody and fragrance of life.

Anonymous

I love the interaction with the kids. They keep me alive in a distinct way.

Robert Trudeau, teacher, in Johnson, All in a Day's Work

Try your Friend before you trust him.

John Newberry, A Little Pretty Pocket-Book

May they who love you be like the sun when it rises in its strength.

Judges 5:31

There's something real clear and direct about the heart-to-heart life of a teacher with the students. That's part of the soul of the business.

Trudeau, in All in a Day's Work

Disruptive children, slow learners, unattractive children—all were challenges for her to show God's love by being the best teacher she knew how to be.

Ruth Beechick, Teaching Primaries

Do not remove a fly from your neighbor's face with a hatchet.

Chinese proverb

A friend will joyfully sing with you when you are on the mountaintop, and silently walk beside you through the valley.

Anonymous

Dear God, Your nice.
—Your Friend, Allen

Children's Letters to God

Friendship is usually a plant of slow growth.

Anonymous

School opened on Wednesday, and that was always one of the happiest days of my life. . . . I looked around and felt back home again. Everybody seemed as glad as I was, scrambling around, not being able to keep still, saying hello to one another and to all the teachers.

Ossie Davis, Just Like Martin

I was the kind of teacher kids came to, for almost anything.

Joseph A. Fernandez with John Underwood, Tales Out of School

Our teaching staff is like a family. We support and care for each other. I have people who listen to me, who know about my ups and downs, and what goes on inside my classroom. It is wonderful to have such deep caring.

Emily Cox, teacher

Friendship . . . lasts only as long as it is nourished with kindness, sympathy, and understanding.

Anonymous

Go often to the house of thy friend, for weeds choke the unused path.

Ralph Waldo Emerson

Kids can smell empty words and false feelings a mile away. On the other hand, there is nothing they know better than the scent of sincerity.

Cartwright and D'Orso, For the Children

VOICES FROM THE CLASSROOM

Among the Children

Before entering the building, the children would line up and recite the Blaine pledge in resounding unison, six hundred little voices echoing up and down the narrow streets of our neighborhood:

"I will act in such a way that I will be proud of myself and others will be proud of me too.
I came to school to learn, and I *will* learn.
I will have a good day."

Cartwright and D'Orso, For the Children

Every week [my science teacher] makes me bring in a new exhibit. I'm going to have a nervous breakdown before I'm six years old!

Sally, in It's a Mystery Charlie Brown *by Charles M. Schulz*

We do hard things here. They fill your brain.

Student quoted by Collins and Tamarkin, Marva Collins' Way

When Jesus was twelve years old he accompanied his parents to Jerusalem for the annual Passover Festival, which they attended each year. After the celebration was over . . . Jesus stayed behind in Jerusalem. . . . He was in the Temple, sitting among the teachers of Law, discussing deep questions with them and amazing everyone with his understanding and answers.

Luke 2:41-43, 46-47

Childhood shows the adult as morning shows the day.

John Milton

Professor Duckett led us in the pledge of allegiance, then everybody sang the Negro national anthem. . . . This song was more important than any lesson in our textbooks. You had to know it letter perfect, like passing a test, and stand up straight and stick out your chest and sing just as loud as you could—or you were dead! The teachers would be busy watching our mouths, checking on who of us was singing and who was faking. They knew how to read your lips, and woe unto the one whose lips weren't moving right. That could get you punished. Your own mother might not speak to you for days, or report you to your father for shaming the family.

Davis, Just Like Martin

Kindness to children and a willingness to conform to the ideal character of childhood are marks of a true Christian.

Petty, Words of Silver and Gold

Abe fooled around a lot. But nothing stopped him from learning. Almost always he was at the head of his class. He was especially good at spelling. One day Abe's class was having a spelling contest. Abe was on one team. His friend Kate Roby was on the other. It was Kate's turn to spell. The word the teacher gave her was *defied.* "D-E-F," she began. The she stopped. Abe knew Kate was trying to decide whether the next letter in *defied* was a *y* or an *i.*

Quickly he pointed to his eye. Kate wasn't the best speller in the room. But she knew when to take a hint! She spelled the word with an *i.*

Margaret Davidson, Abraham Lincoln

Dear God,
When you wrote the bible you made up all the words and spelled them the way you like That is great. Most of the time I do it like that, but I am not doing so good.
—Ron

Children's Letters to God

The school was only 14 by 16 feet. George squeezed in on a long high bench made of rough boards. He thought, *I can hardly move.* Soon he realized, *It is up to me to do the learning, for the teacher is too busy keeping order.*

Fern Neal Stocker, George Washington Carver

Dear Mr. Henshaw,
I am in fifth grade now. You might like to know that I gave a book report on *Ways to Amuse a Dog.* The class liked it. I got an A–. The minus was because the teacher said I didn't stand on both feet.
—Sincerely, Leigh Botts

Beverly Cleary, Dear Mr. Henshaw

Jesus said, "Let the little children come to me, and do not hinder them, for the kingdom of heaven belongs to such as these."

Matthew 19:14, NIV

Miss school? Josh thought. *And today everybody gets his turn in front of the class to tell all he did during the holiday! Oh no. A hundred no's.*

C. Everard Palmer, A Cow Called Boy

After the final bell, I sat at my desk, enjoying the sweet sounds of students discussing the play. As they collected their books, they actually argued with each other about which of Shakespeare's characters was more believable. For an hour I had been a teacher. And it was good.

Johnson, My Posse Don't Do Homework

She sat quietly doing her Sustained Silent Reading.

How peaceful it was to be left alone in school. She could read without trying to hide her book under her desk or behind a bigger book. She was not expected to write lists of words she did not know, so she could figure them out by skipping and guessing. Mrs. Whaley did not expect the class to write summaries of what they read either, so she did not have to choose easy books to make sure she would get her summary right. Now if Mrs. Whaley would leave her alone to draw, too, school would be almost perfect.

Beverly Cleary, Ramona Quimby, Age 8

God sends children for another purpose than merely to keep up the race—to enlarge our hearts; and to make us unselfish and full of kindly sympathies and affections; to give our souls higher aims; to call out all our faculties to extended enterprise and exertion; and to bring round our firesides bright faces, happy smiles, and loving, tender hearts.

Mary Howitt

It was the sheer joy of pleasing me and their teachers and themselves that motivated the kids. They were vessels eager to be filled with happiness and pride. For me to be able to say, "I am so *prouuuud* of you," and to take the kids in my arms and have them feel that joy, and to have them tell me they were proud of us, too—there was no way to measure how much that meant to all of us.

Cartwright and D'Orso, For the Children

Bringing Out the Best

I touch the future. I teach.

Christa McAuliffe, teacher and passenger on The Challenger *space shuttle*

Children are a great deal more apt to follow your lead than the way you point.

Anonymous

While he is keenly aware of his impact as a role model, [Arturo] Barrios also knows there's only so much he can do.

But in the true spirit of a mentor, he accepts this as a challenge and an opportunity. "If I can reach only one kid, then it's okay," he says. "Who knows? It might be the beginning of the beginning."

Thomas W. Evans, Mentors

Children need strength to lean on, a shoulder to cry on, and an example to learn from.

Anonymous

The sacred books of the ancients say: "If you would be holy instruct your children, because all the good acts they perform will be imputed to you."

Montesquieu

All my life I have worked with youth. I have begged for them and fought for them and lived for them and in them. My story is their story.

Mary McLeod Bethune

Just one act of yours may turn the tide of another person's life.

Anonymous

'Tis Education forms the tender Mind;
Just as the Twig is bent, the Tree's inclin'd.

Alexander Pope

And what do we teach our children in school? We teach them that two and two make four, and that Paris is the capital of France. When will we also teach them what they are?

You should say to each of them: "Do you know what you are? You are a marvel. You are unique. In all the world there is no other child exactly like you. In the millions of years that have passed there has never been a child like you. And look at your body—what a wonder it is! Your legs, your arms, your cunning fingers, the way you move! You may become a Shakespeare, a Michelangelo, a Beethoven. You have the capacity for anything. Yes, you are a marvel."

Pablo Casals

Climb high
Climb far
Your goal the sky
Your aim the star.

Inscription on Hopkins Memorial Steps, Williams College

I have given you an example to follow: do as I have done to you.

Jesus, quoted in John 13:15, TLB

Time and chance come to us all. I can be either hesitant or courageous. I can swiftly stand up and shout: "This is my time and place. I will accept the challenge."

Quoted by Collins and Tamarkin in Marva Collins' Way

Those are red-letter days in our lives when we meet people who thrill us like a fine poem, people whose handshake is brimful of unspoken sympathy and whose sweet, rich natures impart to our eager, impatient spirits a wonderful restlessness which, in its essence, is divine.

The perplexities, irritations and worries that have absorbed us pass like unpleasant dreams, and we wake to see with new eyes and hear with new ears the beauty and harmony of God's real world. The solemn nothings that fill our everyday life blossom suddenly into bright possibilities.

Helen Keller

The visions that we present to our children shape the future. They become self-fulfilling prophecies. Dreams are maps.

Carl Sagan

Don't be a carbon copy of something. Make your own impression.

Anonymous

He established a decree in Jacob,
and appointed a law in Israel,
which he commanded our ancestors

to teach to their children;
that the next generation might know them,
the children yet unborn,
and rise up and tell them to their children,
so that they should set their hope in God.

Psalm 78:5-7, NRSV

Not a week goes by that I don't hear from a former student who has something positive to say about the experience they had in my class.

Robert Trudeau, teacher, in Johnson, All in a Day's Work

I have no special gift—I am only passionately curious.

Albert Einstein

Learn well the Motions of the Mind;
Why you are made, for what defined.

Newbery, A Little Pretty Pocket-Book

Rules that control, rather than inform, can kill creativity.

Teresa M. Amabile, Growing Up Creative

Let history talk to you! Every great reform, every grand inspiring movement in the world's history has grown from the defiant stand of determined will against surrounding forces.

C. M. Ward

Life is a journey, not a home.

Petty, Words of Silver and Gold

If you're going to climb, you've got to grab the branches, not the blossoms.

Anonymous

What are we doing here? We're reaching for the stars.

Christa McAuliffe

Let the Teacher Teach . . .

You can't separate yourself as a teacher from yourself as a person. You are all of one piece. And it is good for your pupils that you are. They learn better from a human than from a teaching machine.

Ruth Beechick, Teaching Primaries

The future of our nation depends on the education our children receive, and that education depends on the professional performance and status of our teachers.

Marvin Cetron and Margaret Gayle, Educational Renaissance

I speak truth, not so much as I would, but as much as I dare; and I dare a little the more, as I grow older.

Montaigne

The three *R*s of our school system must be supported by the three *T*s—teachers who are superior, techniques of instruction that are modern, and thinking about education which places it first in all our plans and hopes.

Lyndon B. Johnson

Truth shall overcome,
Truth shall overcome,
Truth shall overcome some day.
Oh, deep in my heart
I do believe
Truth shall overcome some day.

Anonymous

He who knows much speaks with silence.

Amharic Proverb

If a society won't clearly say what it wants from its schools, it won't get any clear performance.

Lester C. Thurow

Successful communication with self and others implies correction by others as well as self-correction.

Jürgen Ruesch

Some people talk in the hall
Some people talk in a drawl
Some people talk, talk, talk, talk
And never say anything at all.

Michael Goode, age twelve, in The Voice of the Children

Well done is better than well said.

Benjamin Franklin

We'll walk hand in hand,
We'll walk hand in hand,
We'll walk hand in hand some day.
Oh, deep in my heart
I do believe
We'll walk hand in hand some day.

Anonymous

The greatest use of life is to spend it for something that will outlast it.

William James

Maybe you'll be one of the lucky teachers who hangs on to the enthusiasm in spite of the system. It happens sometimes, to the ones with fire in their hearts.

Johnson, My Posse Don't Do Homework

She printed his name at the top of the paper and wrote out the last sentence of dictation: *Aesop wrote fables.* Taking Arnold's chin in her hand, she said, "Now let's say the first word together. The *a* is silent so we begin with the *e* sound. Say *ee.* You have to open your mouth in a smile." Arnold repeated the vowel.

"Oh, that's good. Now *sss,* make the sound come through your teeth. Then *ah,* open your mouth wide. And *puh,* make a popping sound with your lips. Now put all the sounds together and say *Aesop.*"

"Aesop," Arnold said.

"Very good. Aesop, Aesop," Ella repeated.

"I know it's Aesop. How many times ya gonna tell me? Wads duh nex' word?"

Ella laughed and mussed his hair. "You're going to do just fine."

Collins and Tamarkin, Marva Collins' Way

There isn't anything wrong with the schools of America that can't be cured.

Fernandez, Tales Out of School

The student is the main character of school. Cause we get the education but they get the money. . . . You know what? I use to think teachers became teachers cause they wanted to help. Why do they have to get paid for it?

Isabel Velez, age twelve, in The Voice of the Children

If everything had turned out the way *I* had intended, I might be growing old teaching geometry in Tucson today.

Joseph Fernandez, Tales Out of School

We must prepare and encourage our teachers to be as concerned with their moral manner as they are with their subject-matter methods.

Gary D. Fenstermacher

A decade ago, American education was undeniably on the decline. Today, though vast amounts of hard work remain, it has begun the long climb back to excellence. . . . Academic perfection may be a long way off, but adequacy can be achieved far sooner and more certainly than most of us would dare to hope.

Cetron and Gayle, Educational Renaissance

Now go, and I will be with your mouth and teach you what you are to speak.

Exodus 4:12, NRSV

What greater or better gift can we offer the republic than to teach and instruct our youth?

Cicero

Beginnings and Endings

Looking back at the dusty trail,
have I come a mile, or just started?

Jerome Holland, age fifteen, in The Voice of the Children

There is a time for everything,
and a season for every activity under heaven;
a time to be born and a time to die,
a time to plant and a time to uproot . . .
a time to tear down and a time to build,
a time to weep and a time to laugh,
a time to mourn and a time to dance,
a time to scatter stones and a time to gather them . . .
a time to keep and a time to throw away,
a time to tear and a time to mend,
a time to be silent and a time to speak.

Ecclesiastes 3:1-7, NIV

The tissue of the Life to be
We weave with colors all our own,
And in the field of Destiny
We reap as we have sown.

John Greenleaf Whittier

Some children breeze through school without causing as much as a ripple on the sea of family life. Others, it seems, carry hurricane-strength turbulence with them as they attack the patience of both the school and the family systems.

William B. Berman, et al., Shaking the Family Tree

This is Mrs. Scarborough's first year at CCS. She decided to teach when she was in ninth grade. . . . If she would leave, she would like a type of law enforcement job.

Rebecca Ledford, age eleven, quoted in a school newspaper

A new teacher has just joined our very wise faculty.

Rachel Perry, age ten, quoted in a school newspaper

Erica . . . sat up in bed, her chin resting on her knees. Today would be her first day in a new school. Her stomach tensed in a tight knot.

Mom came to the doorway . . . [she] understood Erica's fear. Erica didn't know a single person at their new school. She had left so many good friends behind, and here she knew no one.

Kathy Johnson Gale, "Listen to the Bullfrogs"

Use your eyes as if tomorrow you would be stricken blind. And the same for all the other senses. Hear the music of voices, the song of a bird, the mighty strains of an orchestra as if you would be stricken deaf tomorrow. Touch each object you want to touch as if tomorrow your tactile senses would fail. Smell the perfume of flowers, taste with relish each morsel, as if tomorrow you could never smell and taste again. Make the most of every sense. Glory in all the facets of pleasure and beauty Nature in its wisdom has so magnificently provided. Make the most of life while you can!

Helen Keller

Even when her hand was clapped on "bullfrogs" and she had to leave the circle, Erica felt good inside. It would be a while before she had close friends like the ones she left behind, but it was a start.

Kathy Johnson Gale, "Listen to the Bullfrogs"

My child, if you accept my words
and treasure up my commandments within you,
making your ear attentive to wisdom
and inclining your heart to understanding;
if you indeed cry out for insight,
and raise your voice for understanding;
if you seek it like silver,
and search for it as for hidden treasures—
then you will understand the fear of the LORD
and find the knowledge of God.

Proverbs 2:1-5, NRSV

No new group of children will ever take the place
of the one leaving me today.

Murphy, Chalkdust

So I walk away again, and hit the dusty road.

Philip Solomon, age thirteen, in The Voice of the Children

Today is the Tomorrow you worried about Yesterday.

Unknown

Your Life is God's gift to you;
What you do with it is your gift to God.

Unknown

Whatever your years, there is in every being's heart the love of wonder, the undaunted challenge of events, the unfailing childlike appetite for what is next, and the joy in the game of life. You are as young as your faith, as old as your fear, as young as your hope, as old as your despair.

Douglas MacArthur

Without warning, he hugged me again and said, "Goodbye, Miss. J. Have a nice summer. Maybe I'll call you up once or twice so you won't forget me before next year."

"I'd like that very much."

"Hasta la vista."

Johnson, My Posse Don't Do Homework

When you leave here, don't forget why you came.

Adlai Stevenson, to a Princeton University class

It had been a wonderful year for the children. They had achieved in our one-room school as they could not have in schools with large budgets, resource centers, and all sorts of teaching aids and audio visual equipment. The most important reason was that their attitude about school had changed. On the last day of the school year I couldn't get the children out the door.

Collins and Tamarkin, Marva Collins' Way

Every great and commanding moment in the annals of the world is the triumph of some enthusiasm.

Ralph Waldo Emerson

SCHOOL
LIFE

From Reading to Recess

Education is the enthusiastic study of subjects for the love of them and without any ulterior motive.

Charles W. Eliot

I promise you that if somebody had caught me by the shoulder . . . and said to me, "What is your greatest wish in life, little boy? What is your absolute ambition? To be a doctor? A fine musician? A painter? A writer? Or the Lord Chancellor?" I would have answered without hesitation that my only ambition, my hope, my longing was to have a bike . . . and go whizzing down the hill with no hands on the handlebars. It would be fabulous. It made me tremble just to think about it.

Roald Dahl, Boy

At Westside Preparatory School there was nowhere to escape learning. Even the bathrooms had phonics charts tacked on the walls.

Collins and Tamarkin, Marva Collins' Way

All children are educable. They deserve not merely the same quantity of schooling but the same quality, the best education for the brightest children being the best for all.

Marvin Cetron and Margaret Gayle, Educational Renaissance

My book and heart
Shall never part.

New England Primer

Our kids may lose the game, do poorly on tests, or forget their lines in the school play, but they can learn to use failure as a tool rather than a stumbling block.

Nancy Otto Boffo, "Surviving Failure"

Marva beamed. "Now you've got it. Every scholar, every writer, every thinker learned from those who came before. You are all becoming so erudite, we are going to have to dub you MGM—'Mentally Gifted Minors.'"

Collins and Tamarkin, Marva Collins' Way

Some books are to be tasted, others to be swallowed, and some few to be chewed and digested; that is, some books are to be read only in parts; others to be read but not curiously; and some few to be read wholly, and with diligence and attention.

Francis Bacon

Books are the quietest and most constant of friends; they are the most accessible and wisest of counsellors, and the most patient of teachers.

Charles W. Eliot

In class Anna sits up front and concentrates all her attention on the story her teacher is reading. She watches Miss Gross's lips and body language and the pictures in the book.

Bernard Wolf, Anna's Silent World

My four friends and I had come across a loose floor-board at the back of the classroom, and when we prised it up with the blade of a pocket-knife, we discovered a big hollow space underneath. This, we decided, would be our secret hiding place for sweets and other small treasures such as conkers and monkey-nuts and birds' eggs. Every afternoon, when the last lesson was over, the five of us would wait until the classroom had emptied, then we would lift up the floor-board and examine our secret hoard, perhaps adding to it or taking something away.

Dahl, Boy

Imagination is more important than knowledge.

Albert Einstein

O Lord, help me to pass my examination;
O Lord, help the whole school to pass;
O Lord, help the whole world to pass.

Schoolboy's prayer in India

The element that's common to outstanding classrooms is that the teacher has high expectations for herself or himself, and in turn has high expectations for the kids. And nothings stops them. No poor administration, no cut of budget—*nothing stops them.*

Donald Graves

When kids feel right, they'll behave right. How do we help them feel right? By accepting their feelings!

Adele Faber and Elaine Mazlish, How To Talk So Kids Can Learn

Arithmetic is where numbers fly like pigeons in and out of your head.

Carl Sandburg, "Arithmetic"

Letter-writing was a serious business at St. Peter's. It was as much a lesson in spelling and punctuation as anything else because the Headmaster would patrol the classrooms all through the session, peering over our shoulders to read what we were writing and to point out our mistakes. But that, I am quite sure, was not the main reason for his interest. He was there to make sure that we said nothing horrid about his school.

Dahl, Boy

After reading class it's time for recess on the playground. Even though it's a cold December day, Anna chooses to sit on the swings instead of running and playing with her classmates.

At lunchtime Anna munches her peanut butter and jelly sandwich and concentrates on what a classmate across the table is telling her.

Bernard Wolf, Anna's Silent World

Do not provoke your children to anger, but bring them up in the discipline and instruction of the Lord.

Ephesians 6:4, NRSV

When we set a standard and model courteous behavior, students learn that good manners are not ends in themselves, but are aspects of caring and respect.

William J. Kreidler

By three o'clock I was exhausted. The kids burst out of the classroom and spilled out onto the streets. More power to them. They were their parents' responsibility now. I'd done my time.

Faber and Mazlish, How To Talk So Kids Can Learn

Teacher, you have been doing a great job. You are one of the most important people in our society. You deserve a polished red apple, and more.

Beechick, Teaching Primaries

Principals, Parents, and PTA

Education is broader than the schools. The most influential educators are probably parents. What they do, or do not do, plays a crucial role in the lives of their children.

Thomas W. Evans, Mentors

Whatever takes place in school between 9:00 A.M. and 3:00 P.M. is deeply affected by what goes on before and after.

Faber and Mazlish, How To Talk So Kids Can Learn

I'm older and smarter this year, but the questions are harder.

Student to father on school test results, cartoon caption by Bob Schochet

"Thanks again, John, for inspiring us to some good thinking. . . ."
   With that, the principal briskly exited the lounge, leaving behind a beaming John Vroom, his heart too full now to respond, and his mouth too, as it savored the delectable taste of the rum-flavored truffle.

H. K. Zoeklicht, "I Was a Stranger"

Parents and teachers need to join forces and form working partnerships. Both need to know the difference between the words that demoralize and those that give courage; between the words that trigger confrontation and those that invite cooperation; between the words that make it impossible for a child to think or concentrate and the words that free the natural desire to learn.

Faber and Mazlish, How To Talk So Kids Can Learn

It may be difficult to teach a person to respect another unless we can help people to see things from the other's point of view.

Kohei Goshi

All of us, male or female, must work for the day when we are no longer recognized as "new girls on the block" or "old boy insiders," but as respected administrators.

Rosalie B. Icenhower

Since water rises no higher than its source, let us admit that too many American homes are as bare, intellectually and culturally, as Mother Hubbard's cupboard.

Dr. Grayson Kirk

If you spurn wisdom, wise people will spurn you; if you seek wisdom, they will seek you.

Sidney Smith

Optimism breeds enthusiasm.
Positive expectations breed achievement.
Love breeds trust.
Affirmation breeds motivation.
Success breeds self-confidence.
Active involvement breeds active learning.
Faith breeds security.

Lawrence J. Greene, The Life-Smart Kid

Don't just think about your own affairs, but be interested in others, too, and in what they are doing.

Philippians 2:4, TLB

What's most important for all parents is to share responsibility with schools for how well their children learn.

Chester E. Finn, Jr., We Must Take Charge

Dear Mrs. Jackson,
Darryl has been in charge of our class pets this month and all the animals are clean, well fed, and happy.
—Sincerely, Mrs. Bergen

Teacher to parent, quoted in How To Talk So Kids Can Learn

Everybody chooses weapons when dealing with the difficulties of life, and the choice of weapons determines the distinction with which you meet your trials. You can arm yourself with ignorance, indolence, and pessimism—or with wisdom, discipline, and hope.

Eric V. Copage, A Kwanzaa Fable

"For three *A*s, it will be three dollars," Snackman was telling a first-grader who was making a visit to the Corner Store with her mother. Snackman was explaining the possible rewards children could receive from him during report-card time. "But a dollar for an *A* is nothing compared to what you'll get later in life if you're disciplined and study hard." It was a line every school-aged child in the neighborhood knew by heart, for they were obliged to listen to it if they wanted their prize.

Copage, A Kwanzaa Fable

When you educate a man, you educate an individual. When you educate a woman, you educate a whole family.

Chinese proverb

Tales Out of School

In Early America it was the responsibility of the school to teach the "3 R's"—originally Reading, Writing and Religion.

Steven Caney, Kids' America

"What did Mr. Coombes say to you, Mama?"

"He told me I was a foreigner and I didn't understand how British schools were run," she said.

"Did he get ratty with you?"

"Very ratty," she said. "He told me that if I didn't like his methods I could take you away."

"What did you say?"

"I said I would, as soon as the school year is finished. I shall find you an *English* school this time," she said. "Your father was right. English schools are the best in the world."

Dahl, Boy

By the year 2000, all children in America will start school ready to learn. . . . The high school graduation rate will increase to at least ninety percent. . . . Students will leave grades IV, VIII, and XII having demonstrated competence in challenging subject matter, including English, mathematics, science, history, and geography. . . . They will be prepared for responsible citizenship, further learning, and productive employment. . . . U.S. students will be the first in the world in science and mathematics.

Charlottesville summit on education, 1990

Early American schoolhouses were painted red because that was the cheapest color of paint that could be bought.

Steven Caney, Kids' America

Term, holidays, term, holidays, till we leave school, and then work, work, work, till we die.

C. S. Lewis, Surprised by Joy

Oh, Lord! not I; I never read much; I have something else to do.

Jane Austen, quoting John Thorpe in Northanger Abbey

What does education often do? It makes a straight-cut ditch of a free, meandering brook.

Seneca

Learning meant memorization in Early American schools, with little explanation of the lessons provided. After the teacher read an exercise, the class, chanting in unison, would repeat the lesson several times. Each individual pupil would then be made to stand straight and motionless while reciting the lesson from memory.

Caney, Kids' America

There is no royal road to geometry.

Euclid

The secret of teaching is to appear to have known all your life what you have learned this afternoon.

Unknown cynic

Real solemn history, I cannot be interested in . . . the quarrels of popes and kings, with wars or pestilences, in every page; the men all good for nothing, and hardly any women at all.

Jane Austen, Northanger Abbey

"What is the use of a book," thought Alice, "without pictures or conversations?"

Lewis Carroll, Alice's Adventures in Wonderland

Training is everything. The peach was once a bitter almond; cauliflower is nothing but cabbage with a college education.

Mark Twain

"Reeling and Writhing, of course, to begin with," the Mock Turtle replied, "and the different branches of Arithmetic—Ambition, Distraction, Uglification and Derision."

Carroll, Alice's Adventures in Wonderland

I do not tcach, I only tell.

Montaigne

The things taught in schools and colleges are not an education, but the means of education.

Ralph Waldo Emerson

The three foundations of learning: Seeing much, suffering much, and studying much.

Catherall

A teacher who is attempting to teach without inspiring the pupil with a desire to learn is hammering on cold iron.

Horace Mann

The [early American] primer not only taught reading, writing, and spelling but lessons in honor, friendship, and good moral character. The primer was considered an essential tool with which to mold a child's life according to the Christian Ethic. The moral of the lessons was that if you led a good, considerate life you would eventually be rewarded, and if you led a bad life you would be punished.

Caney, Kids' America

Not only is there an art in knowing a thing, but also a certain art in teaching it.

Cicero

Celebrations

The grand essentials to happiness in this life are something to do, something to love, and something to hope for.

Joseph Addison

God be in my limbs and in my leisure.

Motto in Coventry Cathedral

"Valentines aren't just for girls. Valentines are for everybody," said Marvin. "If I were a pilot, I'd draw a great big one in the sky."

Frank Modell, One Zillion Valentines

Everyone takes part in Field Day. It's more than sports and competition. Field Day is a multicultural event. Teachers introduce the kids to the different countries and cultures that are represented on Field Day. Everyone loves the games and events, especially tug-of-war! They cheer each other on. They encourage each other. The kids wish that every day was Field Day.

Eddie Salter, P.E. teacher and basketball coach

A little merry sunshine,
A little wind at play,
And lots and lots
And lots of green,
All for St. Patrick's Day.

Old rhyme

Music stirred the air like a hundred wings.

M. C. Helldorfer, Daniel's Gift

There was a special holiday called Carambano. It is in the verano. When Carambano comes, everyone eats their platos. The people's faces are rojo, azul, and amarillo. On this day people shoot estrellas. There is no sky over this planet. The planet is called Hombre.

Author unknown, quoted in Wishes, Lies, and Dreams *by Kenneth Koch*

Birthdays are remembered in school in Venezuela, and the children sing for the lucky member of the class. Their song is full of bees and nightingales and moonlight and warm with the good wishes that attend birthdays everywhere.

Christine Price, Happy Days

Youth is full of pleasure.

Barnard, The Passionate Pilgrim

First they dress in green.
Then they change their gown
Now, like a queen,
Each one is seen
In red, gold, and brown.

Author Unknown, quoted in The Joy of Words

Thanksgiving can happen any day.

Brian Terpstra, age thirteen

Christmas is celebration; and celebration is instinct in the heart.

Editors, McCall's (Dec 1959)

"Come see our baby," said the mother.
"But I have nothing to give him, just the wooden pipe I play for my sheep."

M. C. Helldorfer, Daniel's Gift

We have talked a little bit about life in the Netherlands. One of their customs is to have an exchange of gifts on St. Nicholas Eve, December 5. I thought it would be nice to celebrate with the Dutch children. We will have a small gift exchange among the children. It is also a Dutch custom to write a small poem or riddle to go along with the gift.

Faye DeVries, third-grade teacher

I would serve mash potatos and gravy with it. And turkey and saled. And candy cains and desert. All of that for Christmas dinner.

Martin, first-grade student

The latkes sizzle sweetly.
The dreidel spins with cheer.
The children's eyes
Are bright tonight
Hanukkah is here!

Anonymous

This Christmas, mend a quarrel. Seek out a forgotten friend. Dismiss suspicion, and replace it with trust. . . . Share some treasure. Give a soft answer. Encourage youth. Manifest your loyalty in word and deed. Keep a promise. Find the time. . . . Listen. . . . Think first of someone else. Appreciate. Be kind; be gentle. Laugh a little. Laugh a little more.

Editors, McCall's (Dec 1959)

The real joy of life is in its play. Play is anything we do for the joy and love of doing it, apart from any profit, compulsion, or sense of duty. It is the real living of life with the feeling of freedom and self-expression. Play is the business of childhood, and its continuation in later years is the prolongation of youth.

Walter Rauschenbusch

Rejoice during your festival. . . . For the Lord your God will bless you in all your produce and in all your undertakings, and you shall surely celebrate.

Deuteronomy 16:14-15, NRSV

POTPOURRI

Wise and Witty Sayings

To know how to suggest is the art of teaching.

Amiel

The secret of education lies in respecting the pupil.

Emerson

Seek not to know who said this or that, but take note of what has been said.

Thomas à Kempis

To receive a proper education is the source and root of all goodness.

Plutarch

The goals of a teacher are high; the responsibility is heavy.

Clare Cherry, Please Don't Sit on the Kids

As each one wishes his children to be, so they are.

Terence

I love the kids. They comfort and encourage me when I am down.

Eddie Salter, P.E. teacher

The teaching is to the teacher, and comes back most to him.

Walt Whitman

I would rather teach two hundred students chemistry than teach anything else.

Chemistry teacher

I have been waiting for this day for eight years.

Jason Holwerda, thirteen, on starting middle-school basketball

I'm not a child. I'm in kindergarten.

Five-year-old girl, quoted in Please Don't Sit on the Kids *by Cherry*

Be your best.

Girl Scouts motto

If you choose to work you will succeed; if you don't you will fail.

Sidney Smith

To love the beautiful, to desire the good and to do the best.

Moses Mendelssohn

Our character comes from who we are, not from what we do.

Don Holwerda, Christian school superintendent

Few things are harder to put up with than the annoyance of a good example.

Mark Twain

I strive to be thoroughly prepared.

Steve Irwin, middle school teacher

Just as every apple, no matter how different it is on the outside, has a star within its core, so does every child.

Kay Kuzma

No piano teacher could possibly be as fun as you!

Rachel DeMoss, saying good-bye to her piano teacher

What will a child learn sooner than a song?

Alexander Pope

One of my beginners (a first grader) was playing a very easy version of the "Ode to Joy." I told her that this was written by a very famous composer and asked if she had ever heard of Beethoven. She very seriously replied, "Yes, but I didn't know that dogs could write music."

Jean Rohrer

You can make music of a sort with white keys only, but for true harmony you need the black keys also.

James E. Kivegyir Aggrey

Mr. Koch is a very well-dressed poetry book walking around in shining shoes.

Tara Housman, fourth grader, describing her teacher in
Wishes, Lies, and Dreams *by Kenneth Koch*

Young people, like trees, need to be planted in an environment where they can grow to bring forth fruit.

Promotional brochure

A tree is a nobler object
than a prince
in his coronation robes.

Alexander Pope

I give you sound learning,
so do not forsake my teaching.

Proverbs 4:2, NIV

My business is not to remain myself, but to make the absolute best of
what God made.

Robert Browning

Centerville High School's seniors had a sublime send-off at graduation exercises. After diplomas were granted, a senior girl rose and solemnly said: "Now, will you please rise for the benediction and continue rising while the class sings our alma mater."

Quoted by Herbert V. Prochnow in A Speaker's Treasury

Stickers and Other Rewards

"It means exactly what it says," [Miss Kemp] said. "You're to think of a special compliment for each person in this class, and please don't groan"—a lot of people did anyway—"because this is the assignment for the *year.* You have all year to think about it, and next June, before the last day of school, you'll draw names from a hat and think of more compliments for just that one person."

Barbara Robinson, The *Best* School Year Ever

Fix your thoughts on what is true and good and right. Think about things that are pure and lovely, and dwell on the fine, good things in others.

Philippians 4:8, TLB

That's using the old noodle!

Sticker award caption

I just get "Wow!" and "Good" and that stuff. I've never really had a compliment for my work from my teacher.

Third grader

I'd wish to have Mrs. Wiener through Elementary School, Junior High school, and College.

Annie Clayton, in Wishes, Lies, and Dreams *by Koch*

Antigone, you are a natural-born leader. You are at the top of your class and I want to congratulate you.

Sixth-grade teacher

What a brain you have!

Sticker award caption

Gratitude is the sign of noble souls.

Aesop

So far I had thought up compliments for six people, including Alice. For Alice, I put down "Important."

Barbara Robinson, The *Best* School Year Ever

I pin up good work on their bulletin board. I tell them: "You really did a good job."

Homeschool teacher

Let me be a little kinder, let me be a little blinder
To the faults of those about me; let me praise a little more.

Author unknown

Oh the bliss and the wonder of being with the family once again after all those weeks of fierce discipline! Unless you have been to boarding-school when you are very young, it is absolutely impossible to appreciate the delights of living at home. It is almost *worth* going away because it's so lovely coming back.

Dahl, Boy

A is for all right!

Sticker award caption

In my faithfulness I will reward them.

Isaiah 61:8

When others reassure us that we are appreciated, worthwhile, liked, capable, and accomplished, our self-esteem increases.

Cherry, Please Don't Sit on the Kids

He labors vainly who endeavors to please every person.

Latin proverb

There were signs and posters about fires and firemen everywhere; all the blackboards said "Woodrow Wilson Elementary School, Speed and Safety Winner!" Kids were making bookmarks and placemats, and writing poems and stories about our big accomplishment. We didn't even have hot dogs and hamburgers at lunch—we had Fire Dogs and Smokey Burgers.

Robinson, The *Best* School Year Ever

You're a star!

Sticker award caption

She's a pleasant, kind friend to her classmates.

Elementary teacher, on a student's second-grade report card

This year there was no big surprise about what we would do on the last day. It was up on the blackboard—Compliments for Classmates—and we had each drawn a name from a hat and had to think of more compliments for that one person.

Robinson, The *Best* School Year Ever

To be meaningful, praise should not be overused.

Cherry, Please Don't Sit on the Kids

I had finally thought of a word for Albert. Once you get past thinking fat you can see that Albert's special quality is optimism, because Albert actually believes he will be thin someday, and says so. Another word could be determination, or even courage. There were lots of good words for Albert.

Robinson, The *Best* School Year Ever

Touching hearts,
Encouraging minds
And building on
Curiosity with creativity.
Helping and leading by godly
Example. Rich the
Reward: hope for the future.

Elsa Stewart, Glad Heart Originals

I remembered Joanne Turner's paper—"Cheerful, good sport, graceful, fair to everybody." I had wondered who that was.
It was me.

Robinson, The *Best* School Year Ever

Congratulations on reaching your goal!

Sticker award caption

Praise should not be confused with flattery.

Cherry, Please Don't Sit on the Kids

To the girl who swiftly finished her math test I said, "You went through all those examples like a mouse nibbling cheese."

Elementary teacher, quoted in How To Talk So Kids Can Learn
by Adele Faber and Elaine Mazlish

Those who sow righteousness get a true reward.

Proverbs 11:18, NRSV

Helpful Hints

By keeping your child's cerebral engine stoked, you can significantly improve the likelihood that she'll make good, rational choices in this dangerous world of ours. Keep shoveling coal into the furnace. There's room for more, and there's plenty of track ahead!

Greene, The Life-Smart Kid

Don't be afraid to turn things upside down and approach your classroom from some new angles.

Cherry, Please Don't Sit on the Kids

Children want more than just a friend in their teachers; they want them to teach.

Diane E. Papalia and Sally Wendkos Olds, A Child's World: Infancy through Adolescence

To waken interest and kindle enthusiasm is the sure way to teach easily and successfully.

Tryon Edwards, The New Dictionary of Thoughts

A little girl from one of our schools in San Francisco went one day to visit a public school and immediately noticed that the desks were dusty. She said to the teacher, "Do you know why your children don't dust and instead leave everything in a mess? Because they don't have pretty dust-cloths. I wouldn't want to clean without them."

Maria Montessori, The Child in the Family

No school is perfect for every child at every age.

Harlow G. Unger, "What Did You Learn in School Today?"

Teachers must be careful not to make promises that they may not be able to keep, and they must always keep the promises they make.

Cherry, Please Don't Sit on the Kids

Early instruction in truth will best keep out error. Some one has well said, "Fill the bushel with wheat, and you may defy the devil to fill it with tares."

Tryon Edwards

It is obvious that teachers have to make conscious efforts to accept all their pupils, even those whose value systems differ most from their own.

Papalia and Olds, A Child's World: Infancy through Adolescence

The true object of education should be to train one to think clearly and act rightly.

Henry J. Van Dyke

Get wisdom, get understanding;
do not forget my words or swerve from them.

Proverbs 4:5

The one exclusive sign of a thorough knowledge is the power of teaching.

Aristotle

Never educate a child to be a gentleman or lady only, but to be a man, a woman.

Herbert Spencer

Trust breeds trust.

Cherry, Please Don't Sit on the Kids

Girl Scout Soup
A whole lot of activities
A heap of creativity
Lots of friends (assortments of personalities enhance flavor)
Add enough fun to thicken
Typically brewed in the great outdoors but different interesting tastes are possible in different locations
TRY THEM ALL!
Leftovers make great memories!

Carrie Kauzlarich, 1996 Girl Scout Calendar

I am only one, but I am one. I can't do everything, but I can do something. And what I can do, that I ought to do, and what I ought to do, by the grace of God, I shall do.

Edward Hale

Faith, Hope, and a Sense of Humor

God has something special for your child to contribute to this world. Not all children have physical beauty, or skills, or keen mental ability. Some children are born with physical handicaps or brain damage, but regardless of this, every child has a star of potential.

Kay Kuzma, Vibrant Life

The education of the human mind commences in the cradle.

T. Cogan

The years of childhood are brief. They should be years filled with wonder and the beautiful magic of play, of growing, of doing, of knowing.

Cherry, Please Don't Sit on the Kids

There are three things that remain—faith, hope, and love—and the greatest of these is love.

1 Corinthians 13:13, TLB

It is not conceivable that our culture will forget that it needs children. But it is halfway toward forgetting that children need childhood. Those who insist on remembering shall perform a noble service.

Neil Postman, The Disappearance of Childhood

Every child needs to be encouraged to experience the pleasures of sports, song, dance, theater, and art without worrying about having to be the star athlete or a musical genius or the class actress or the family artist.

Faber and Mazlish, How To Talk So Kids Can Learn

A child who cannot keep his balance dares neither to walk nor use his arms for fear of falling; he goes forward only uncertainly. But if he can learn to keep his balance, he will run, jump and turn right and left.

Maria Montessori, The Child in the Family

Some people are too tired to give you a smile. Give them one of yours, as none needs a smile so much as he who has no more to give.

Author unknown, quoted in The Joy of Words

Life is mysterious.

Montessori, The Child in the Family

The way I see it, there's always a chance for deep-down goodness.

Sue Diaz, on difficult students, in Instructor (Nov/Dec 1995)

What am I doing to increase the sum of hope in this world? What am I doing to nourish the sense of purpose that founded this nation and made it strong? What am I doing to teach someone else what I have learned?

Dr. Arthur Burns

To help all the children during a handwriting exercise, I suggested that they have a "beauty contest" and circle the most beautiful letter on their paper to be the winner. Some children felt they had two equally beautiful letters. In that case both letters were declared "co-winners."

Faber and Mazlish, How To Talk So Kids Can Learn

"Everyone who looks at you," my mother said, "knows that you are going away to a Public School. All English Public Schools have their own different crazy uniforms. People will be thinking how lucky you are to be going to one of those famous places."

Dahl, Boy

Each day in the Christian school classroom, teachers take youngsters and young people on field trips of faith. God calls them to teach our children to know him through learning to see God's sovereign hand everywhere and in everything. This is the teacher's calling. This is the teacher's gift.

Sheri D. Haan, "Field Trips of Faith" Christian Home & School (Dec 1995)

Endurance produces character, and character produces hope, and hope does not disappoint us.

Romans 5:4-5, NRSV

Teacher time must be seen as precious—limited and inelastic.

Clarence LeBlanc

I cultivated times for faculty members to be with each other. They met together every day for devotions and a time of sharing. Wonderful things happened when these teachers gathered. . . . They encouraged each other, they listened, they shared their successes and failures, they grew to depend on each other, and they learned to not take themselves too seriously.

Dr. Jeff Hall, former elementary school principal